Pensions -Youi ~i.vill

An explanatory guide

Fourth Edition

Cherrill Braithwaite BA
of Godwins Limited

(Based on a text by
John V Wilson FCA and
Bryn Davies BSc (Econ), FIA
of Bacon & Woodrow)

Tolley Publishing Company Limited
A UNITED NEWSPAPERS PUBLICATION

Whilst every care has been taken to ensure the accuracy of the contents of this work, no responsibility for loss occasioned to any person acting or refraining from action as a result of any statement in it can be accepted by the author or the publishers.

Published by
Tolley Publishing Company Ltd
Tolley House
2 Addiscombe Road
Croydon CR9 5AF England
081-686 9141

Printed and bound in Great Britain by
Butler & Tanner Ltd,
Frome and London

ISBN 0 85459 530-9

Contents

CONTENTS

CONTENTS

About this book

The third edition of Your New Pensions Choice was published in March 1988. In 'About this book' at that time the authors, John Wilson and Bryn Davies, commented 'Writing this book has proved to be a little like trying to shoot at a moving target'. This has turned out even truer than they thought. Within three years it has been necessary to produce a fourth edition - and the story is still not at an end! As you read you will realise that there are some pensions questions which still cannot be answered.

In producing the fourth edition, retitled Pensions - Your Choice, I have followed very closely the content and style of the third edition, but despite the excellent work done by John Wilson and Bryn Davies, the book has needed considerable up-dating. Largely this is due to new legislation and regulations; partly it is because matters that were still mainly theory in March 1988 are now schemes we are accustomed to using.

The main changes in content are the promotion of pension transfers to a chapter on their own account and the inclusion of a chapter which describes some of the alternative investments to pensions for savings.

I should like to thank all those people whose help I have received, and especially to pay tribute to John Wilson and Bryn Davies. Their work has made the production of the fourth edition much easier than it might have been.

April 1991

Cherrill Braithwaite
Godwins Limited
Braithcliff House
Kingsmead
Farnborough
Hampshire GU14 7TE

1
Introduction

Note on fourth edition

This fourth edition has been updated to include changes introduced by the Finance Act 1990, the Budget Proposals 1991 and the Social Security Act 1990.

A pensions revolution has begun in the UK and is continuing to develop. In July 1988 important new ways opened up for you to provide for your retirement. These include personal pensions and additional facilities to enable you to increase your pension yet remain a member of your employers' pension scheme.

Everyone now has alternatives to consider and choices to make. This is particularly true if you are employed.

This short book first explains the recent and new legislation, how and when it is being introduced and how it affects existing pensions law and practice.

It next sets out clearly the various alternatives which are available to you. To find out, all you have to do is to decide which of the five categories of employment listed below is relevant to you.

Finally, it gives you independent, unbiased advice to help you make the right pension choice in your present circumstances and taking into account your likely career pattern in the years ahead.

No previous knowledge of pensions or pensions terms is needed when reading this book. Technical terms, indicated with an asterisk*, are explained in 'boxes' as they first arise in the text and again in the glossary to be found at the end of the book.

Please note that throughout this book the phrase *'pension scheme'* is only used to mean an *occupational pension scheme* i.e. one run by your employer (or perhaps within your employer's trade or profession) and which you and your fellow employees can join, either now or when you become eligible. Similarly, personal pensions are always referred to as *'personal pension plans'* , to distinguish them from occupational schemes.

How this book can help you

The structure of this book is set out below:

Chapter 2 explains the pensions background and sets the current scene. It also summarises the changes which are taking place and which will affect pension schemes in the future.

Chapter 3 tells you which of the alternative ways of providing for your pension will actually be available to you. This will depend upon whether you are now:

(a)   employed, and a member of a *contracted-out pension scheme**;

(b)   employed, and a member of a contracted-in pension scheme (i.e. one that has not been contracted out of SERPS*);

(c)   employed, but not (yet) a member of any pension scheme;

(d)   self-employed, responsible for your own national insurance contributions and income tax on earnings; or

(e)   unemployed, for any reason.

---

*A *contracted-out pension scheme* is one whose members have been contracted-out of the *State Earnings Related Pension Scheme* (SERPS) (see Chapter 7).

A scheme can only be contracted-out if it is approved by the Inland Revenue and if it satisfies certain conditions laid down by the Occupational Pensions Board (an independent government appointed body). These can now include either the provision of a *guaranteed minimum pension* ('GMP') to members (approximately equal to that they could expect to receive under SERPS) or minimum contributions.

If you are in any doubt as to whether your pension scheme is contracted-out or contracted-in, ask your employer to tell you.

Having found out in Chapter 3 which alternatives are open to you, you can decide which of the next three chapters you need to study carefully.

Chapter 4 deals in detail with personal pension plans, setting out their advantages and disadvantages.

Chapter 5 explains the rules on *AVCs** setting out their advantages and disadvantages.

> *AVCs* are additional voluntary contributions which a member of a pension scheme can make to increase his or her pension at retirement.

Chapter 6 deals with your employer and your present pension scheme. It considers how the present changes may affect your employer's scheme and some of the courses of action he might take.

Chapter 7 is a reminder about how the present State Pension Schemes work.

Chapter 8 sets out the choices open to you if you are changing your job. Once again your choices will depend on whether you are moving to a new employer or becoming or ceasing to be self-employed. They will differ depending on the type of pension scheme of which you were a member.

Chapter 9 covers a range of subjects such as *pension mortgages**, early and late retirement and the position in situations such as prolonged absences from work or death in service. It also describes the earnings cap and considers its possible affects.

> *Pension mortgages* are loans for house purchase or improvements, repayable from lump sums provided by pension arrangements (see Chapter 9).

Chapter 10 considers some of the private savings schemes available for regular monthly savings and compares them with your pension scheme or personal pension plan as a method of providing for retirement.

1 -- INTRODUCTION

Chapter 11 is perhaps the most important in the book. It sets out to give independent, unbiased advice to help you make the most sensible choice taking into account factors such as your age, your length of service with your present employers, the likelihood of your changing jobs in the years ahead, the terms of your employer's present pension scheme and how much you have to contribute now to your pension scheme and whether you will be better off in or out of SERPS etc. Some examples of typical employment situations are given, covering cases in which the pensions choice is easy to make and others in which the choice is marginal and much more difficult.

The *Appendices* which follow cover:

A   Effect of inflation.
B   Retirement annuities (see Chapter 2).

Finally never make a hasty decision on this important subject before studying carefully all the pros and cons of the alternatives open to you. The wrong decision now may cost you or your dependants thousands of pounds in lost pensions or life assurance benefits in the years to come. However, do not put off taking a decision, just because the subject seems so complicated. In doubt or in cases of difficulty always take professional advice.

2

The background: where we are now

This chapter summarizes the current pensions scene and provides the necessary background for the rest of this book.

Why you should provide for your retirement

You need to save or provide for retirement for the obvious reason that you will lose your earnings from your work when you retire. At the same time as putting money aside for your pension, it is sensible also to cover other events such as death or long-term ill-health so as to provide financial protection for your spouse and other dependants.

How you can provide for your retirement now

(a)   for the employee

The available methods are:

(1)   **The two State schemes:**

(i)   The *flat rate scheme* provides a pension of an amount fixed by the government each year, regardless of the level of your pre-retirement earnings. From April 1991, the flat rate pension is £52 per week for a single person, £83.25 per week for a married couple if the wife was not a contributor. If both husband and wife were contributors, the maximum combined pension is 2 x £52 = £104 per week.

These figures assume that both husband and wife had (if appropriate) full contribution records.

Whether the wife's pension was paid for her by her own contributions or her husband's, it is now treated as her own income for tax purposes. This may mean that there is no income tax to pay on her part of the pension.

(ii)   The *State Earnings Related Pension Scheme* (SERPS), provides an additional pension based on your pay between 'band earnings' for national insurance purposes. The band is changed each year (see page 25).

Every employee has to participate in the flat rate scheme by paying national insurance contributions deducted from pay. Your employers also have to pay national insurance contributions on your behalf.

However, you can be contracted-out of SERPS by being a member of a contracted-out pension scheme run by your employers. Both you and they then pay national insurance contributions at the lower contracted-out rate.

There is more about these two State schemes in Chapter 7.

(2)   **A pension scheme run by your employer**

Known more fully as occupational pension schemes, these are usually schemes which are approved by the Inland Revenue. For a pension scheme to be approved it must meet certain requirements of the Inland Revenue, including limits on benefits provided under the scheme. Only an approved pension scheme enjoys the following taxation privileges.

(i)   Tax relief is given on employee contributions by deduction from income before income tax is calculated.

(ii)   Tax relief is given to employers by allowing their contributions as a deduction for tax purposes.

(iii)   Income and capital gains of the pension scheme are tax-free.

(iv)   Tax-free lump sums (within limits) can be paid by the scheme to members on retirement. Pensions paid are treated as taxable income of the recipient. (However, they are treated as earned income, which may be important if there is an extra tax charge on investment income in the future.)

Pension schemes can be *contracted-out* of SERPS (as explained in Chapter 1), or *contracted-in*.

They will be either *non-contributory** or *contributory**.

*Non-contributory means that only the employer pays contributions towards the scheme, usually as a percentage of pay.

*Contributory means that both employer and employee pay contributions, usually as a percentage of pay.

Pension schemes will be *insured* or *self-administered*. An insured scheme is one under which the contributions are paid to an insurance company. In return, the insurance company undertakes to invest the contributions and to pay some or all of the benefits provided under the scheme. Most large pension schemes are now self-administered. The contributions are paid to the trustees of the scheme for direct investment, under the advice of specialist in-house or external investment managers.

Pension schemes will also be either *defined benefit** schemes or *defined contribution** schemes.

**A *defined benefit* scheme is one under which the pension benefits are fixed at your retirement regardless of the investment performance of the scheme. The benefits are usually calculated as 1/60th or 1/80th of your pensionable pay (see below), immediately prior to your retirement, for each year of 'pensionable service' (employment by your employer which counts towards your pension entitlement). This is why defined benefit schemes are usually known as *'final salary '* schemes.

Any contribution by you as an employee is usually a fixed percentage of your pensionable pay (the pay on which your pension will be based, which in some schemes may be your normal pay less an amount such as the lower earnings level for national insurance), but your employers undertake to put into the scheme **whatever is necessary** to provide the scheme's members with their defined benefits.

> *A *defined contribution* scheme is in contrast one in which the contributions for either or both employer and employees are at agreed rates. The ultimate benefits are dependent on the value of the fund built up by contributions paid and income from its investments during your membership of the scheme. The fund is used to purchase you a pension on your retirement. These schemes are usually known as *'money purchase'* schemes.

You can add to your pension benefits from a pension scheme by making additional voluntary contributions (AVCs) provided that your AVCs plus your ordinary contributions as a scheme member (if any) do not exceed 15% of your salary.

You may pay AVCs either to your employer's scheme or to a separate arrangement offered by, for example, an insurance company. These are called free-standing additional voluntary contributions (FSAVCs).

AVCs and FSAVCs are explained more fully in Chapter 5.

(3)   Retirement annuities

If you are an employee, you can only contribute towards one of these policies if you are not a member of a pension scheme. (This is known as 'non-pensionable employment'.) Unlike a pension scheme run by an employer, under which the amount of the eventual benefits is limited by the Inland Revenue, the benefits from a retirement annuity are limited by the maximum contribution which may be paid.

Contributions have to be made under a special insurance policy. They will then accumulate free of income tax and capital gains tax to provide a cash fund from which an annuity must be purchased on your retirement. The policy can also provide death benefits, and a tax-free lump sum on retirement which must not exceed three times the remaining pension.

Since 1 July 1988 it has not been possible to take out a new retirement annuity, but there is more information about existing policies in Appendix B which were called section 228 policies.

(4)   Personal pensions

Personal pension plans are a relatively new form of tax-efficient pension plan, introduced with effect from 1 July 1988.

Personal pension plans are similar to Retirement annuities in that the benefits are limited by the maximum contributions which may be paid (although the limits are higher for personal pensions if you are over 35). Contributions accumulate free of income tax and capital gains tax to provide a fund from which an annuity must be purchased on your retirement. The policy can also provide death benefits and a tax-free lump sum on retirement which must not exceed one-quarter of the accumulated fund.

However, there are a number of differences:

(i)   If you are an employee and one of your Personal Pension Plans is an *appropriate** one, you may use it to contract out of SERPS.

*An *appropriate personal pension* is one which, by satisfying certain conditions under the Social Security Act 1986 and being approved by the Occupational Pensions Board, enables the contributor to the plan to be contracted-out of SERPS (see Chapter 4).

(ii)   An employer who does not operate a pension scheme may pay contributions to a personal pension plan for you, provided that his contributions and yours combined do not exceed the limit you are permitted.

(iii)   If you leave an employer, you may take with you the value of the pension earned in your employer's scheme, and transfer it to a personal pension plan. (This is described more fully in Chapter 8.)

(iv)   If you are already a member of your employer's pension scheme, but you feel it would suit you better to have a personal pension plan, you may opt out of the scheme and take out a personal pension instead.

Remember that, although your employer may contribute to your personal pension, he will probably not wish to do so if he already offers his employees a pension scheme.

Personal pension plans are described in more detail in Chapter 4.

(5)   Private savings

You may make your private savings through a variety of different investments. However, no other investment offers quite the same advantages as a pension scheme or personal pension plan.

The characteristics of some types of private savings are considered in Chapter 10.

(b)   for the self-employed

The available methods for the self-employed are:

(1)   The *State flat rate scheme* (see above) towards which you have to pay Class 2 National Insurance contributions. You cannot participate in SERPS as a self-employed person.

(2)   *Retirement annuities* are available as for an employee (see (3) above) provided you had taken one out before 1 July 1988 and it can accept further contributions.

(3)   *Personal pension plans* are available as for an employee (see (4) above).

(4)   *Private savings* are available as for an employee (see (5) above).

Current developments

(a)   Social Security Act 1990

The Social Security Act 1990 contained various measures designed to protect members of final salary schemes.

(1)   *Limited Price Indexation** [LPI] for pensioners

From 'A Day' (a date yet to be set) pension schemes will have to provide

LPI on all final salary pension above GMP (see page 2) which you earn in your employment from then until you retire. Any associated money purchase benefits, such as AVC's or the proceeds of a transfer (see Chapter 8) will not have to have LPI.

> *Limited Price Indexation* means that pensions being paid must increase each year for life at the same rate as inflation, as measured by the Retail Prices Index, subject to a maximum of 5% each year.

If you are a member of a final salary scheme that has a surplus on or after 'A Day', that *surplus** must be used to add LPI to all final salary pension (over GMP) earned before 'A Day'. An employer will not be able to stop making contributions, or take a refund from the scheme, until all final salary pensions carry LPI. This includes preserved pensions for people who have left, pensioners who have already retired and spouses or children.

> *Surplus* occurs when a scheme has more money than it needs to pay the pensions it has promised. *Surplus* can be worked out in different ways, but always in such a way that members can be sure the scheme will have sufficient money to meet its promises. The exact basis which will be used when a scheme has a *surplus* for this purpose has not yet been announced.

(2)   *Statutory revaluation** for leavers

If you left an employer's pension scheme after 1 January 1986, the scheme has to add *statutory revaluation* until pension age, but only on that part of the pension earned after January 1985.

If you leave after 1 January 1991 the scheme will have to add *statutory revaluation** until pension age on all the pension, whether it was earned before or after 1 January 1985.

> *Statutory revaluation* is worked out at pension age as a once and for all increase in line with retail prices since you left or, if less, at 5% a year compound. It applies to final salary pension over GMP, but not to money purchase pensions.

A scheme which is being wound up must provide the compulsory statutory revaluation up to pension age and LPI on pensions in payment in the same way as a continuing scheme before it can be closed down finally.

If the scheme does not have enough assets to provide the promised pensions with these compulsory increases, then the employer has to provide the money. Obviously, if the scheme has to be wound up because the employer is insolvent, there is unlikely to be sufficient money available but the rules will give protection to the members if the scheme is wound up in any other situation.

It is important to remember that this rule applies only to final salary schemes. Money purchase schemes are not affected.

As a further protection, if an employer is insolvent, then an independent trustee must be appointed. This trustee has to be completely independent: he must not have any previous connection with the employer or with the scheme itself. His job is to look after the interests of the scheme members.

(3)   *The Pensions Registry*

The Registry will hold details of all occupational pension schemes and personal pension plans. The details will be supplied by employers and by the providers of personal pension plans. This service will make it possible for people retiring to trace any pensions which they cannot locate.

For example, a company for which you worked thirty years ago may have been taken over several times since you left. Once the Registry is set up you will be able to use it to make contact with the present trustees of the scheme and find details of any pension to which you are still entitled.

Schemes registering have to pay a levy, which is used to pay for the Registry, OPAS (see below) and the Ombudsman (see below).

(4)   *The Occupational Pensions Advisory Service* [OPAS]

This service has in fact existed for some years, but as a charity. The

Social Security Act 1990 has made it into an official organisation. It has arranged for OPAS to have more funds so that the service can be extended.

If you have a problem with your pension and have not been able to obtain a satisfactory answer from the scheme's trustees or from the personal pension provider, then you may contact OPAS.

(5)   *The Pensions Ombudsman*

In most cases, OPAS will be able to help you to sort out the problem. However, if you still feel that you have not been treated fairly, even with the aid of OPAS, then you will be able to refer your case to the Ombudsman. He will have the power to demand that documents be produced and evidence given. His decisions will be legally binding, so that if he decides in favour of a member, the scheme trustees or the personal pension provider will have to obey his decision and *vice versa*. The Ombudsman will be able to accept enquiries from 2 April 1991.

(b)   **The Barber Case**

Mr Barber was made redundant when he was 52. Because he was more than 10 years from his scheme's pension age of 65 he was not offered an immediate pension. Women of the same age, whose retirement age was 60, would have been offered an immediate pension.

Sex discrimination over pay is illegal under European Community Law. Mr Barber claimed that his pension was a form of pay. He sued his former employer for sex discrimination.

Eventually the case was submitted to the European Court of Justice, which decided that Mr Barber was right in claiming that the pension from the employer is a form of pay. From the 17 May 1990 therefore it is illegal for pension schemes to discriminate between men and women in this way. This means, among other things, that a pension scheme will no longer be able to have different pension ages for men and women. Unfortunately, many of the other details are not clear yet, and may not be made clear until a similar case is submitted to the European Court.

The possible effects of the Barber Case are considered in more detail in Chapter 6.

3
The choices available

The alternatives available to you under the present legislation depend upon whether you are now or are likely to be:

(A)   Employed and a member of a pension scheme which is contracted-out of SERPS, or

(B)   Employed and a member of a pension scheme which is not contracted-out of SERPS, or

(C)   Employed but not a member of a pension scheme, either because:

●   the employer has no pension scheme, or

●   the employer has a pension scheme but you have decided not to join it, or

●   your age or length of service or terms of employment prevent you from joining, at least for the time being.

        You are also in this category if you are a member of a scheme run by your employer which provides **only** death in service benefits and/or widow's or other dependant's benefits.

(D)   Self-employed, or

(E)   Unemployed.

The choices available under each of these categories are explained on the following pages.

Advice to help you make the best choice in your present and likely future circumstances is given in Chapter 11.

(A)   Employed and a member of a contracted-out pension scheme

You can do one of the following:

- Remain a member and take no further action.

- Remain a member but increase your pension benefits by making or increasing additional voluntary contributions (AVCs) within your pension scheme. AVCs are described more fully in Chapter 5.

- Remain a member but increase your pension benefits by making FSAVCs outside your pension scheme. FSAVCs are described more fully in Chapter 5.

- Opt out of membership of your pension scheme:

  (a)   in favour of a personal pension plan. You will be entitled to a 2% incentive payment from the DSS up to 5 April 1993 if your personal pension plan is an appropriate one (see Chapter 4), and you have not been in your present contracted-out employment for more than 2 years, or

  (b)   make no provision for pension other than through the State schemes.

Personal pension plans are explained fully in Chapter 4 and the State schemes in Chapter 7.

(B)   Employed and member of a contracted-in pension scheme

You have exactly the same choices as in (A) with two important additions.

- If you opt out in favour of an appropriate personal pension plan, you will be entitled to a 2% incentive payment from the DSS until 5 April 1993. Personal pension plans and this incentive are explained fully in Chapter 4.

- As an alternative, you may contract-out of SERPS through an FSAVC.

(Note: This category includes members of an employer's scheme which provides **only** death in service benefits and/or widow's or other dependant's benefits.)
You can either:

- continue with one or more **retirement annuity policies** (see Chapter 2) if you took them out before 1 July 1988. These policies will provide you with a lump sum and pension on retirement. Lump sums under retirement annuity policies may be greater than under personal pension plans, but see Appendix B for more information about retirement annuities, or

- take out one or more **personal pension plans,** one of which could be an appropriate personal pension plan to enable you to contract out of SERPS and possibly also enjoy the 2% DSS incentive payment. This does not prevent you from continuing with any existing retirement annuity policies provided your total premiums still remain within the limits allowed by the Inland Revenue for personal pensions, or

- join the **pension scheme** when you become eligible and then have the options under categories (A) or (B) available to you. You would then have to cease contributing to your retirement annuities or personal pension plans, which would be treated as paid-up. **You cannot both be a member of an employer's scheme and pay premiums to a retirement annuity or personal pension plan in respect of the same job** (unless the personal pension plan only accepts payments from the DSS), or

- continue with any **retirement annuity policies** but take out an appropriate personal pension policy to enable you to contract out of SERPS and possibly also enjoy the 2% DSS incentive payment, or

- **do nothing.** If you do nothing, you will have to continue to contribute to SERPS.

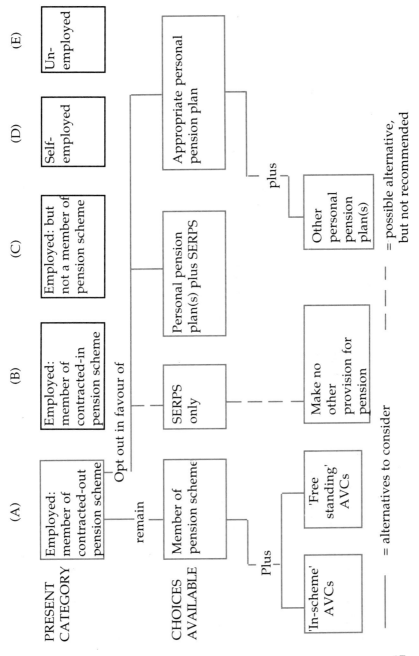

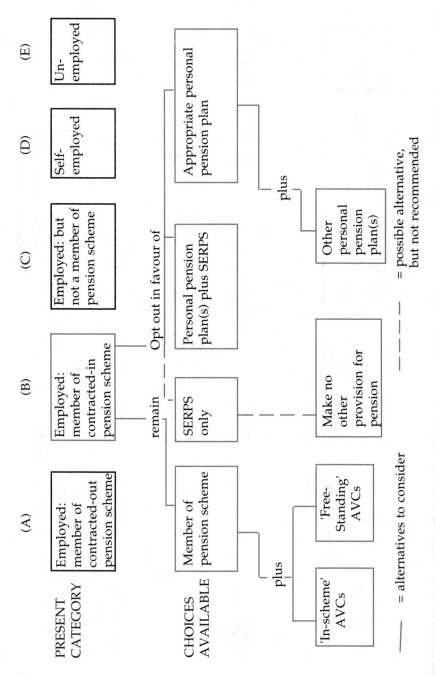

PRESENT CATEGORY

(A) Employed: member of contracted-out pension scheme

(B) Employed: member of contracted-in pension scheme

(C) Employed: but not a member of pension scheme

(D) Self-employed

(E) Un-employed

CHOICES AVAILABLE

remain

Opt out in favour of

Member of pension scheme

SERPS only

Personal pension plan(s) plus SERPS

Appropriate personal pension plan

plus

'In-scheme' AVCs

'Free-Standing' AVCs

Make no other provision for pension

plus

Other personal pension plan(s)

——— = alternatives to consider

– – – = possible alternative, but not recommended

18

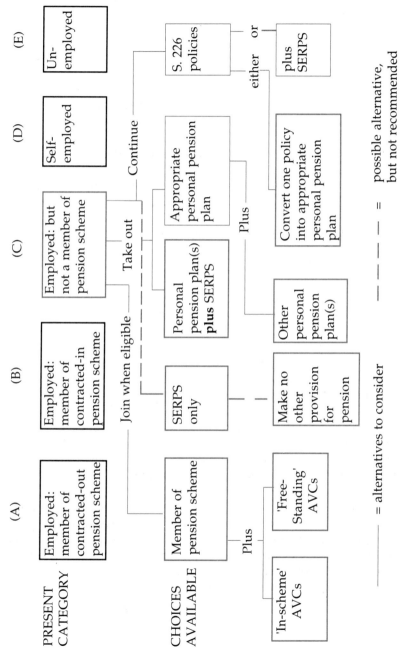

| PRESENT CATEGORY | (A) Employed: member of contracted-out pension scheme | (B) Employed: member of contracted-in pension scheme | (C) Employed: but not a member of pension scheme | (D) Self-employed | (E) Un-employed |

CHOICES AVAILABLE

- Member of pension scheme — Plus — 'In-scheme' AVCs / 'Free-Standing' AVCs
- Join when eligible
- SERPS only — Make no other provision for pension
- Take out — Personal pension plan(s) **plus** SERPS / Appropriate personal pension plan — Plus — Other personal pension plan(s) / Convert one policy into appropriate personal pension plan
- Continue — S. 226 policies — either / or — plus SERPS

——— = alternatives to consider

– – – = possible alternative, but not recommended

3 -- THE CHOICES AVAILABLE

Retirement annuities are explained more fully in Appendix B, personal pension plans in Chapter 4 and SERPS in Chapter 7.

(D)   Self-employed

You may:

- continue any **retirement annuity policies** you already have and/or

- take out one or more **personal pension plans,** none of which can be an appropriate personal pension plan. This is because, as a self-employed person, you cannot participate in SERPS. Therefore, you cannot contract-out of it, or

- take no further action and rely on the basic State pension only.

(E)   Unemployed

If you are unemployed for any reason you cannot take out a personal pension plan because you have no *'net relevant earnings'**.

> * *Net relevant earnings* are, broadly, earnings from employment or as a self-employed person your earnings less deductions (other than personal allowances) which are made to arrive at your taxable income for income tax purposes.

If you were previously in employment and were a member of a pension scheme you will be entitled when you retire to the benefits secured to date from your own and your employer's contributions. Your rights in these circumstances are summarised in Chapter 8.

Similarly if you were previously in employment or were previously self-employed, you will have to treat as paid-up any personal pension plans or retirement annuities to which you were contributing, until such time as you have net relevant earnings again or until you retire. (This must be after age 50 for a personal pension plan or age 60 for a retirement annuity, except for some special occupations.)

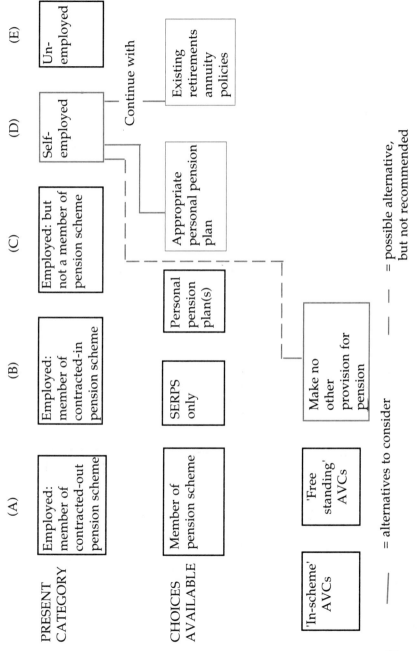

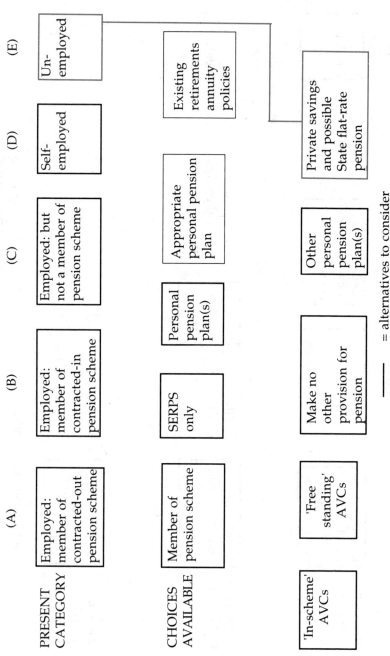

	(A)	(B)	(C)	(D)	(E)
PRESENT CATEGORY	Employed: member of contracted-out pension scheme	Employed: member of contracted-in pension scheme	Employed: but not a member of pension scheme	Self-employed	Un-employed
CHOICES AVAILABLE	Member of pension scheme	SERPS only	Personal pension plan(s)	Existing retirements annuity policies	Private savings and possible State flat-rate pension
	'In-scheme' AVCs	Make no other provision for pension	Appropriate personal pension plan		
	'Free standing' AVCs	Other personal pension plan(s)			

――― = alternatives to consider

You also cannot participate in SERPS if you are unemployed. However, it is possible to continue to pay national insurance contributions voluntarily to ensure your entitlement to certain benefits will continue. **The position is extremely complex and you are strongly recommended to consult your local DSS office for help and advice if you are in this situation.**

4
Personal pensions

Introduction

Personal pension plans were introduced from 1 July 1988. They were introduced by the government principally to encourage those who are in employment but who are not members of a pension scheme to make additional provision for their retirement, and, if they wish, to contract-out of SERPS by making their personal pension plan an **appropriate** one (see below). They are not available to people who continue to be members of their employer's pension scheme if that scheme is contracted out of SERPS.

However, the government also decided that after 6 April 1988 it should no longer be possible to make membership of pension schemes compulsory for employees. This means that pension scheme members may now opt out in favour of personal pensions. The arguments for and against opting out are discussed more fully in Chapter 11.

Appropriate personal pension plans

Certain personal pension plans are described as 'appropriate'. They enjoy two particular advantages:

(1)   An appropriate personal pension enables you as an individual to contract out of SERPS. At present the terms for contracting-out of SERPS are relatively favourable but do depend on your age and sex. **It will normally be worth serious consideration if you are aged under 50 (men) or under 42 (women)**, for the reasons explained in Chapter 11.

If you take out an appropriate personal pension plan, you and your employers will pay the full normal rate of national insurance contributions each week or month. However, the DSS will then pay direct to your personal pension plan (see below) a sum equal to the contracting-out rebate, which is the difference between the full and contracted-out rate of national insurance contributions. In additional they will pay a sum equal to the income tax relief due to you on your share of those contributions to your personal pension plan plus the incentive addition (see (2) below).

This is not as complex as it sounds. You may more readily understand how the DSS contributes towards your appropriate personal pension plan if you look at the example on pages 30 and 31.

(2) As an encouragement to contract out of SERPS, the DSS will also make an additional incentive payment to your appropriate personal pension plan until 5 April 1993 **unless** you have been in your present contracted-out job for the two years or more immediately before you start the plan. (In other words, you will not be able to obtain this incentive payment if you have been a member of a contracted-out pension scheme, or would have been a member of such a scheme had you been eligible to join but chose not to, for the past two years or more).

The amount of this DSS incentive is 2% of your 'band earnings'* or £1 per week if greater.

> * *Band earnings* is pay falling between the lower and upper earnings limits for national insurance purposes (£52 and £390 per week respectively between 6 April 1991 and 5 April 1992).

If you started an appropriate personal pension plan on or before 5 April 1989 you may have been able to backdate its start to 6 April 1987 and thus receive the DSS incentive for up to six years to 5 April 1993.

Appropriate personal pension plans have to satisfy certain conditions under the Social Security Act 1986 and be approved by the Occupational Pensions Board.

Married women (and widows) paying national insurance contributions at the reduced rate cannot take out an appropriate personal pension plan. If you are self-employed you cannot take out an appropriate personal pension plan. This is because you have not been contributing to SERPS which is only open to employees, and so you cannot contract out of it. But if you subsequently become an employee, you will then be able to take out an appropriate personal pension.

The payment of appropriate personal pension plan contributions is dealt with later. First, some other general points which apply to all personal pension plans.

Who can take out a personal pension plan and when

If you are aged under 75 you can contribute towards one or more personal pension plans at any one time. You are not, however, allowed to contribute if:

(a)   you are at the same time a member of a pension scheme unless that scheme **only** provides lump sum benefits on death and/ or widow's or other dependants' benefits, or

(b)   you have retired and are drawing a pension from a company of which you were a *controlling director**.

---

* Broadly, a *controlling director* is one who, together with members of his immediate family, controls more than 20% of the voting shares of the company.

Only one plan can be an appropriate one and the total contributions payable on all the plans must be within the limits explained below.

You may take out an appropriate personal pension plan if you are a member of a pension scheme which is contracted in to SERPS. This appropriate personal pension plan may only receive the national insurance contributions as set out below. Neither you nor your employer may make any additional contributions.

Capped earnings

The Finance Act 1989 introduced a limit on the amount of earnings which may be taken into account for providing pension benefits. This limit is often called the 'earnings cap'. For the year from April 1990 to April 1991 the cap was set at £64,800 and from 6 April 1991 it is £71,400. There is more information on the 'earnings cap' in Chapter 9.

Whether or not it may be sensible to opt out of your pension scheme in favour of a personal pension plan is discussed in Chapter 11.

Portability

Your personal pension plan is fully portable. It belongs to you, and you can take it with you from job to job **without loss.**

Contribution limits

The contributions you pay each year to personal pension plans are fully deductible from your earnings for income tax purposes. They must be within the limits set by the Inland Revenue as stated below:

Age at start of the tax year (6 April)	% of capped earnings
Up to 35	17.5
36 to 45	20.0
46 to 50	25.0
51 to 55	30.0
56 to 60	35.0
61 to 74	40.0

These limits do **not** include the contributions by the DSS to appropriate personal pension plans but do include any contributions to existing retirement annuities.

Your employers may also contribute towards your personal pension plan (although they are not under any obligation to do so). The contributions may be paid:

(a)   entirely by you, or

(b)   entirely by your employers, or

(c)   by you and your employers between you

provided that the total contributions from both of you do not exceed the limits set out above.

If your employers do contribute, their payments will be deductible for tax purposes as an expense of their business. Their contributions are not treated as your income for income tax purposes.

You may also pay additional contributions and claim any unused tax relief for the previous six years. Contributions paid use up first the available relief for the current tax year, the excess then being set off against any unused relief for the previous six years (taking relief in the earliest year first).

This is called 'carry forward', because you are **carrying forward** the unused relief.

You may also choose, at any time before 5 April, to have the contribution you have paid treated as if it had been paid in the previous tax year, (provided that you had not already made your maximum contributions for the previous year, of course). This is called 'carry back', because you are **carrying back** the contribution.

Neither 'carry forward' nor 'carry back' can be used by your employers. They are only available to you as an individual.

Benefits limits

At your retirement the fund built up through all the contributions to your personal pension plan over the years (plus reinvested income and capital growth) must be applied as follows:

(*a*)   Up to 25% can be paid to you as a tax-free cash lump sum on retirement.

However, none of the fund created by the DSS minimum contributions to an appropriate personal pension plan can be taken as a lump sum. All of that fund must be used to purchase an *annuity**.

* An *annuity* is an income for life. You pay (or the provider of your personal pension plan pays) a capital sum to an insurance company which then pays you an income for as long as you live.

(b)   The remainder of the fund must be used to purchase an annuity
from an approved insurance company on retirement between
the ages of 50 and 75. The amount of the annuity will depend
on:

- interest rates at the date of purchase;

- your age at retirement;

- your sex (but see below); and

- the type of annuity you choose.

Under a personal pension plan you have freedom to decide how you
would like your pension to be paid. You may choose that it should
continue to be paid to your widow or widower or that it should
increase each year. Either of these options will reduce the amount of
pension you receive when compared with a pension payable by level
amounts for your lifetime only.

Special rules apply to the annuity benefits secured by the DSS
contributions. These must be used to provide an annuity from age 65
or later for men and age 60 or later for women, calculated on 'unisex'
rates (i.e. the same rates for men and women of the same age).
Furthermore, the annuity must increase annually by 3% or the rise in the
Retail Prices Index (whichever is less), and in most cases, must
provide a 50% pension for the life of your widow or widower.

Payment of contributions to an appropriate personal pension plan

The way in which contributions to an appropriate personal pension
plan reach the plan is complicated.

Firstly, **you** will only pay direct to the personal pension provider the
premium you have chosen to pay. If you are an employee you will pay
the contribution **less** income tax at the basic rate (currently 25%). This
is similar to the scheme operated by the Inland Revenue to give
mortgage interest tax relief at source (the 'MIRAS' scheme). If you pay
tax at a higher rate, you will receive the additional relief by adjustment
to your tax code. (Currently there is only one higher rate of tax of 40%).

If you are self-employed you will pay your personal pension contributions gross i.e. without deducting any tax before you pay. You will receive your tax relief later, by adjustment to your tax bill.

As previously explained, you and your employer will still have to pay the full rate of national insurance contributions each week or month when you are paid your net wage or salary.

Secondly, the insurance company will invest the gross amount of the premium. It will then reclaim from the Inland Revenue the basic rate tax relief which has been deducted.

Thirdly, the DSS will pay direct to your personal pension plan after the end of each tax year after employers have sent in their annual returns:

(a)   the difference between the full national insurance contributions you and your employer have paid and the contracted-out, lower rates of national insurance. This difference, known as the contracted-out rebate, is 5.8% of band earnings for the tax years 1988/89 to 1992/93, plus;

(b)   the tax relief at the basic rate of income tax due to you on your proportion of the rebate in (a) above, plus (if payable);

(c)   the DSS incentive (normally 2% of band earnings) referred to earlier.

Here is an example to show how the payment of contributions will work in practice:

Example
Assume Mr Andrews, who is an employee earning £250 per week, (equivalent to approximately £1,080 per month) decides to contribute £50 per month to an *appropriate personal pension plan*. Assume also that the basic rate of income tax is 25%, the national insurance band earnings are as stated on page 25 and that Mr Andrews is entitled to the 2% DSS incentive.

Mr Andrews will pay each month to the plan	£38.50
The insurance company will reclaim from the Inland Revenue	£12.50

The DSS will pay, in due course, to the plan:

(a)	Both the employers' and the employee's national insurance rebate (3.8% + 2% = 5.8%) on Mr Andrews' band earnings (which are £250 - £52 = £198)	£11.48
(b)	Income tax relief due on the employee's national insurance rebate (2% of Mr Andrews' band earnings @ 25% = 25/75 x 2%)	£ 1.32
(c)	The 2% DSS incentive on Mr Andrews' band earnings = 2% of £198	£ 3.96
		£16.75

The pension provider receives:

From Mr Andrews	£38.50
From the Inland Revenue	£12.50
From the DSS (£16.76 x 52)÷12 = £72.63	£72.63
Total monthly payment to the personal pension provider	£123.63

Notes

(a) The figures for the national insurance rebate are worked out by the week, but most pension plan providers take contributions monthly, so the example shows the equivalent monthly contribution.

(b) In this example, the £123.63 works out at 11.41% of Mr Andrews' pay, of which he contributes only 3.55%. But he will lose future SERPS benefit in respect of this employment.

(c) The maximum amount which the DSS will contribute to an appropriate personal pension plan in 1991/92 will be £1,488. This is worked out as shown in the example, but based on £338 per week which is the difference between lower and upper band earnings for 1991/92.

Payment of other personal pension plan contributions

These will follow the same pattern as explained above except that there will be no payments from the DSS. Thus, if Mr Andrews decided to invest only in an ordinary personal pension plan he would still pay £38.50 per month and the insurance company would claim £12.50 from the Inland Revenue, to give a total premium of £50.

For all types of personal pension plans, **any contributions paid by the employer** will go to the plan **gross**, with no deduction of tax.

Providers of personal pensions

Only the following are allowed to offer personal pension plans:

Investment type organisations: Life assurance companies
Unit trusts
Friendly societies

Deposit type organisations: Banks
Building societies

These organisations operate under the control of various 'regulatory bodies' as follows:

Type of Organisation	Appropriate Personal Pensions	Ordinary Personal Pensions
Investment	Securities and Investment Board rules (under Financial Services Act)	Securities and Investment Board rules (under Financial Services Act)
Deposit	DSS regulations	Bank or Building Society regulations

The charges being made have to be disclosed by the plan provider

Illustrations for personal pension plans issued by investment type organisations will have to be given in accordance with two bases laid down by LAUTRO (The Life Assurance and Unit Trust Regulatory Organisation, an organisation approved by the Securities Industry Board.)

There are a number of safeguards created to ensure that personal pension plans are properly and securely managed. There is always an element of risk, though, in any investment and if you decide to begin a personal pension plan you should take particular care in choosing the provider.

How to choose a personal pension plan provider

If you decide you want to invest in a personal pension plan you next have to choose which provider (e.g. insurance company, unit trust, bank, building society or friendly society) you will trust with your money. You also have to decide how you wish your personal pension plan to be invested.

The four most common types of investment fund on offer are:

(a) Cash/Deposit: The amount accumulated at retirement is equal to the original contributions plus interest at a rate which will be fixed from time to time in line with rates paid on money held on deposit. These rates are likely, in the longer term, to be unattractive when compared with those available on other investments, but are more certain.

Almost all providers offer a cash or deposit option.

(b) With profits: This type of fund is only available from life assurance companies. To the initial value of the policy bonuses are added each year. Future rates of bonus are not guaranteed, but once a bonus has been 'declared' and added to the

33

investment, it will not be withdrawn. In addition, most companies pay a final or 'terminal' bonus. This enables you to share in the performance of the company's investments if they have done better than expected. This means that it is impossible to promise terminal bonus in advance.

(c) Managed Fund :

In its true form, a managed fund is only available from a life assurance company. It is called a 'managed' or 'mixed' fund, because the managers of the life company's pension funds decide how much of the fund will be invested in cash or fixed interest investments, how much in property, how much in stocks and shares in the UK and how much in stocks and shares overseas. They will also alter the balance between these investments from time to time.

A managed fund gives you the opportunity to have your money managed professionally even if your contributions are small. You will also benefit from all the types of investment within the fund which would not be practicable if you were investing for yourself unless you had a very substantial sum of money available. This is done by issuing you with a number of 'units' in the fund, which is itself spread between the various types of investment.

The rate of growth in the fund cannot be guaranteed, so the value of the units will fall from time to time as well as rise. However, in the medium to long term the variety of investment types should make it possible to achieve good reasonably steady growth.

(d) Equities:

Equities are stocks and shares. Investment through an equity fund or a unit trust gives you the opportunity to invest in those companies whose shares are bought and sold on the stock market and so to share in their prosperity. The companies may be based in the UK or they may be overseas. You are able to choose between general equity funds, UK or international, or you may prefer a more specific selection: for example, a Japanese fund or a fund which invests only in smaller companies.

The value of your units will fluctuate if there are movements in the stock market, which may even fall dramatically at times. Over the longer term, however, equity investment has always shown good growth which has beaten the rate of inflation. There cannot, however, be any guarantees.

These are just brief outlines of the most common forms of investment used for personal pensions. There are others. For instance, if your contributions are large enough (on their own or with fellow employees') you may have a personal pension plan under which you yourself choose the investments.

Whatever type of personal pension plan you choose, you will have to decide how much risk you are prepared to take. For example, to replace the guaranteed benefits from the State scheme you will probably want the level of security given by a with-profits policy. If you are paying contributions in addition to contracting out of SERPS, your decision will probably be most affected by how old you are now and when you expect to retire.

Don't forget the general rule that the greater the potential growth in an investment, the higher the risk will be.

The following table may help:

(a) Cash/Deposit: Very safe, but unlikely to give good rate of growth in the medium to long term. Suggested timescale is 0-5 years.

(b) With profits:	Still safe, because bonuses once declared cannot be withdrawn, but potential for growth limited by the security offered. Suggested timescale is 5-15 years.
(c) Managed Fund:	No actual guarantees, but spread of investments should give reasonable prospects for growth whilst offering some protection against stock market falls. Suggested timescale is 10-20 years.
(d) Equities:	No guarantees, but should provide good, if uneven, growth over the longer term. Suggested timescale is 15 years or more.

You do not have to invest the whole of your contributions in the same fund. Subject to the conditions laid down by the provider, you may choose several of the funds which it offers. Nor do you have to use only one provider. There is no limit to the number of personal pension plans you have provided that only one of them is an appropriate personal pension plan and that the total contributions do not exceed the limits shown on page 27.

An important point to remember is that you cannot judge a plan by the projections of possible benefits which will be given to you. They are only estimates, and have to be made on a standard basis (see page 32). What you can look at is the return which has been achieved in the past. Some providers have been able to achieve consistently above-average results. It is this consistency of performance for which you should be looking. It is no good picking the fund which has been at the top for one year only for an investment which may be going to last twenty-five years or even more.

Past results offer no guarantee of what will happen in the future.

You must also remember that a large part of the expenses of most plans is taken up by the commission paid to the agent who sells you the plan. Some providers do not pay commission, which suggests that they may be better value, even if they are not recommended by an agent who relies on his or her income from commission. However, this is not automatically the case.

When anyone tries to sell you a personal pension there are a number of questions you should ask before signing anything. Even after you have signed a proposal you will have a 'cooling off' period of 14 days during which you can change your mind without penalty. If the provider is a life assurance company or a unit trust house, it will also have to supply you with information about the amount of your contribution which will be spent on commission and charges.

The questions to ask of anyone selling you a personal pension plan are the following:

- Are you tied to selling the products of only one provider or are you advising that this is the most suitable personal pension plan for me out of those available?

- What will be the amount of money in my personal pension plan after one, two and five years assuming I continue to contribute at present levels, compared to the contributions I will have paid? [This information should appear on the formal illustration from the provider.]

- How much can I expect my pension to be at my normal retirement age compared with my estimated salary at that time?

- What happens if I retire early for any reason?

- What happens to my personal pension plan if I die before retiring or when I die after retirement?

- How does your investment performance record over the past five and ten years compare with the projections in your proposal to me?

- What variety of investment funds do you offer and how easy is it to switch between them?

- What happens if I cease contributing to my plan with you within one, two, five or ten years?

- How simple is it for me to change the level of contributions or for my employer to begin contributing?

- Exactly what will happen if I change my job and want to continue my plan?

Transfers of previously accrued benefits to and from personal pension plans

Pension rights which have been accrued in a pension scheme can be transferred to a personal pension plan, subject to certain safeguards. It will also normally be possible to transfer accrued rights from personal pension plans back to pension schemes provided the scheme agrees.

The whole question of how changing jobs can affect your pension is discussed in Chapter 8.

Advantages of personal pension plans compared with final salary pension schemes

- Portability - no loss on change of job.

- Visible fund, growing year by year.

- There is no limit on pension benefits, only on contributions to the personal pension plan. So full advantage can be gained from particularly favourable investment conditions.

- Your personal pension plan fund benefits if, as in the past ten years, investment returns (interest, dividends and capital growth) have been high.

- Freedom to choose your plan provider and to change from time to time.

- Can provide attractive pension benefits for younger people.

- May enable you to contract out of SERPS if you wish and thus also enjoy the DSS incentive up to 5 April 1993.

- Lump sum cash option on retirement may be greater than that available from your pension scheme.

- Freedom to choose how you wish your pension to be payable.

Disadvantages of personal pension plans compared with final salary pension schemes

- No sort of guarantee by your employer about the level of your retirement benefits.

- Your pension will be less certain because it will not be related to your final salary.

- Your pension at retirement will depend on two uncertain factors:

  (*a*) how well your money has been invested **up to your retirement.**

  (*b*) annuity rates **at the date of your retirement.**

- + Death in service and ill-health benefits will probably be an extra cost to you, if you leave your present pension scheme or choose not to join.

- + Total contributions being paid in are likely to be less than under a pension scheme, as most employers will not wish to contribute towards them. Except for the very young this in turn will normally mean that less benefit emerges.

- You are solely responsible for ensuring that your contributions are increased as you get older in order to ensure that your pension provision increases as your earnings increase.

- The limitations on contributions which can be made to personal pension plans.

- + You may not be allowed to rejoin your present employer's pension scheme if subsequently you want to, anyway probably not on favourable terms.

- + Any commission to an agent selling you a personal pension plan will affect the amount invested in your personal pension plan.

- + Administrative charges will be made by the personal pension plan provider. These can sometimes be a significant proportion of the contributions paid. In pension schemes, similar charges are usually borne by the employer.

- Personal pension plans are likely to be poor value if contributions are only made for a short period due to administrative charges and commission.

- Delay in the receipt of premiums from the DSS and Inland Revenue.

+ = Also applicable to **money purchase pension** schemes as compared with **personal pension** plans.

5

Additional voluntary contributions (AVCs)

Since April 1988 all pension schemes have had to offer 'in-scheme' AVC facilities to their members, except that if your employer has more than one pension scheme, only one of those schemes has to offer the facilities.

There are two Inland Revenue limitations on AVCs:

(*a*)   The employee may not contribute more than 15% of his earnings to pension schemes. This limit includes both compulsory contributions to the employer's scheme and any AVCs.

(*b*)   The total benefits provided by the AVCs and the pension scheme taken together must not exceed the benefit limits prescribed by the Inland Revenue (but see below).

AVCs within these limits are fully allowed as deductions from your income for income tax purposes. Providing your pension scheme rules permit, you may vary the amount and timing of AVC contributions, subject of course to the Inland Revenue limits. Your employer can refuse to accept 'in-scheme' AVCs below 0.5% of your taxable earnings or three times the National Insurance lower earnings limit (£52 per week from April 1991) in any tax year, whichever is the higher.

Free-Standing AVCs (FSAVCs)

If you are a member of your employer's pension scheme and you wish to make extra contributions, you do not have to make them through the AVC facilities offered by the employer. Instead you may pay into an FSAVC. The limits on total contributions are the same as for 'in-scheme' AVCs.

5 -- ADDITIONAL VOLUNTARY CONTRIBUTIONS (AVCs)

These arrangements are offered by life assurance companies and building societies. You pay your FSAVC net of basic rate income tax. Any higher rate tax relief will be given to you by adjustment to your tax code.

Provided your FSAVC is less than £200 per month, it will not be necessary to provide any information about your benefits from your employer's pension scheme. If you wish to pay more than that the organisation providing the FSAVC will need to obtain details of your existing benefits from the pension scheme.

An AVC or FSAVC cannot provide you with an additional cash lump sum at retirement (unless it was taken out before April 1987). When you retire, the whole of the fund accumulated must be used to purchase a pension. However, it may be possible to take into account the pension from your AVC or FSAVC when calculating the maximum cash lump sum you may take from the pension scheme itself. You should ask the person who runs your employer's scheme about this possibility.

If the pension scheme provides pension benefits and lump sum in fixed proportions, then the 'in-scheme' AVC may do the same.

If you are a member of a contracted-in pension scheme, you may use your FSAVC to contract out of SERPS if it meets the requirements of an appropriate personal pension plan approved by the Occupational Pensions Board (see Chapter 4). However, in this case there will be no tax relief on the employee's national insurance rebate, so it will be better to use an appropriate personal pension plan.

If you reach retirement and the combined proceeds of your employer's scheme, your AVCs or FSAVCs and any pension benefits you may have had from a previous employer exceed Inland Revenue limits, then you will be able to take a refund from your AVC or FSAVC. However, there will be a tax charge on the proceeds, to allow for the tax relief you received on the premiums and the tax that you did not pay on the investments during the period up to retirement.

AVCs and FSAVCs do offer a very tax efficient method of saving. They are compared with other forms of saving in Chapter 10.

6

Your employer

Chapter 2 described some of the changes to pension schemes being brought about by the Social Security Act 1990 and the Barber case.

Social Security Act 1990

It is important to remember that revaluation and limited price indexation only apply to final salary pensions. They are likely to prove expensive for schemes which do not already provide increasing pensions at 5% a year.

- Some employers in this position may not feel able to commit themselves to an increased cost. They may decide to discontinue their final salary schemes and replace them with money purchase schemes or group personal pension plans. Both these types of pension provision enable an employer to decide in advance how much he is prepared to pay. The eventual benefits will then depend on the level of the contributions, the return on the investments and the annuity rates at retirement.

- Some employers may decide to wind up their final salary schemes and not replace them. Their members will then have to rely on SERPS or take out personal pension plans to provide pension benefits in respect of their future service.

- Some employers may redesign their schemes, so as to provide a lower starting pension, but a higher rate of increase on the pension. In this case, members may well wish to start or increase AVCs or FSAVCs.

- Some employers will accept the changes without altering benefits even though this may mean they have an increase in contributions, which could be shared with employees.

It is also important to remember that a pension provided by an employer is part of your overall remuneration package. If the scheme is improved, other rewards may be reduced. But if the scheme benefits are reduced or the scheme is discontinued, employees will be looking for compensation if the employer's costs have been cut and his profits improved.

The Barber case

The Barber case affects all pension schemes which have different normal retirement ages for men and women, whether final salary or money purchase.

The precise meaning of the decision by the European Court of Justice is still not clear, but employers are required to take action or face lawsuits. Broadly speaking, the options are as follows:

(*a*) To equalise retirement ages at 65 for men and women. This is the cheapest option, but it is unlikely to be popular with women who were expecting to qualify for pension at 60.

(*b*) To equalise retirement ages at 60 for men and women. This would probably be the most popular with members, but it is also the most expensive. Not all men will necessarily be happy to lose five years' earnings.

(*c*) To pick a common age between 60 and 65. This approach combines the advantages and disadvantages of (a) and (b).

(*d*) Introduce flexible retirement ages - the 'decade of retirement' approach. This will enable men and women to choose when they want to retire between ages set by the scheme. Whatever age is chosen, the pension payable will be equal for a man or a woman.

Although it is essential to equalise, the decision is complicated by uncertainty over state pensions. Until the government announces when and how state retirement ages will be equalised, employers risk setting different dates under their schemes and being forced to adjust again in the near future.

Equal retirement ages will also have the effect of equalising the benefits available before normal retirement age, whether on early retirement or for any other reason.

7
Pensions from the State

This book would be incomplete without some further explanation of the pensions available through the State.

There are two principal pension rights:

(*a*)   The basic State flat-rate or 'old age' pension.

(*b*)   A pension from the State Earnings-Related Pension Scheme (SERPS).

There are many other pensions such as older person's pensions, pensions to war widows and widows under industrial death benefits and the old graduated pension scheme.

The basic State flat-rate pension

This pension is available to everyone who has made enough national insurance contributions (or who is the widow of a contributor). It is not payable before men reach age 65, women age 60.

Rates per week from 6 April 1991

Single Person :		£52.00
Married Couple - wife non-contributor:	husband	£52.00
	wife	£31.25
Married Couple - both contributors:	husband	£52.00
	wife	£52.00

The State Earnings-Related Pension Scheme (SERPS)

SERPS began in 1978, when the Social Security Pensions Act came into force.

All employees who do not belong to a contracted-out pension scheme have to participate in SERPS. However, as explained in earlier chapters, it is possible for individuals to contract-out of SERPS through an appropriate personal pension plan, perhaps taken out instead of being a member of a pension scheme.

Until April 1988, only final salary pension schemes were able to satisfy the OPB's requirements on minimum benefits so as to enable them to contract-out. However, now money purchase schemes may also contract-out if they meet the OPB's alternative requirements.

Pension benefits under SERPS

When introduced SERPS provided a pension equal to **one-eightieth** of revalued average band earnings i.e. between the lower earnings limit and upper earnings limit, for each year in the scheme, **up to a maximum of 20 years** i.e. a maximum of 20/80ths or one quarter of *revalued average band earnings**. If the employee had completed more than 20 years by retirement date, the pension was based on the average of the best 20 years' revalued band earnings, not necessarily the final 20 years'.

> **Revalued average band earnings* means that earnings are revalued in line with the increase in national average earnings each year, and so are virtually inflation-proofed.

SERPS is only payable at the State retirement age (currently still 65 for men, 60 for women) but may be deferred until 70 and 65 respectively.

Under the Social Security Act 1986, the government, concerned at the long-term cost of SERPS, reduced these benefits for all those retiring after March 2000. From then on, the pension will begin to be based on **lifetime** average earnings (not the best 20 years). The maximum benefits will fall over a period of 10 years to one-fifth, instead of one-quarter, of revalued average earnings.

It will be obvious from this that SERPS represents better value in return for contributions paid by employees due to reach State retirement age before the year 2000 (i.e. men now aged 55 or over and women now aged 50 or over), than for younger employees.

As contributions to SERPS are made *via* national insurance contributions, they do not attract tax relief like contributions to pension schemes or personal pension plans. Higher paid employees will have even more need to make additional provision for their retirement since SERPS benefits are only based on 'band earnings', not on full earnings.

You can find out your SERPS pension entitlement by completing the form contained in the DSS leaflet NP38 and posting it to Newcastle. (NP38 is obtainable from local DSS offices.) Within a few weeks, the DSS will provide you with an 'additional pension' statement showing:

(a)   the amount of your SERPS pension earned so far (or to previous 5 April) at today's values;

(b)   an estimate of what SERPS will provide as pension if you continue working to the State pension age; and

(c)   an estimate of the SERPS pension at that date if your future earnings increase faster than prices.

The statement will be accompanied by an explanatory leaflet (NP39).

8

Changing jobs or leaving service before retirement

If you leave your employer before your normal retirement date, for whatever reason, and you are not taking early retirement (see Chapter 9) you will have to decide what to do with your pension benefits.

Your options will differ according to whether you are in one or other of the following categories:

- A member of a pension scheme moving to an employer who operates a pension scheme.

- A member of a pension scheme moving to an employer who does not have a pension scheme or becoming self-employed.

- A member of a pension scheme but not moving to another job.

- You have a personal pension plan (or retirement annuity) and are moving to an employer who operates a pension scheme.

- You have a personal pension plan (or retirement annuity) and are moving to an employer who does not have a pension scheme, or are becoming self-employed.

- You have a personal pension (or retirement annuity) but are not moving to another job.

Member of a pension scheme moving to an employer who operates a pension scheme

You have three options open to you which are as follows:

8 -- CHANGING JOBS OR LEAVING SERVICE BEFORE RETIREMENT

(1)   To leave the pension benefits you have earned in the scheme of your old employer.

(2)   To take a transfer value to your new employer's scheme.

(3)   To take a transfer value to a personal pension policy (or special 'buy out' policy (used to be called a 'S 32 Buy out' policy).

(1)   **Leave your benefits in the scheme**

If the scheme is a final salary scheme, the amount of benefit will be based on your length of service with your employer and your earnings at the date you left.

If the scheme is a money purchase scheme, then contributions will cease, and the value of the contributions already paid will continue to grow until you reach retirement age.

(2)   **Take a transfer value to a new scheme**

If the scheme you are leaving was a final salary scheme, the transfer value will be the value now of the benefits described in (1) above.

If you are leaving a money purchase scheme, then it will be the value now to which the contributions already paid have grown.

If you transfer to a new money purchase scheme, then the extra pension you will receive will be based on the amount to which your transfer payment has grown by the time you retire.

The situation if you transfer to a final salary scheme is more complicated. It is difficult for anyone except an actuary to assess the benefits offered and decide whether the transfer provides good value. It may be preferable to consider transfer to a personal pension plan.

(3)   **Transfer to a personal pension plan**

You may choose to have your transfer value paid to a personal pension plan. The pension payable to you at retirement will depend on the growth (interest, dividends and capital gains) in the sum paid to the personal pension plan.

At retirement you will have the same options as under an ordinary personal pension plan (see Chapter 4). You will be able to take up to 25% of the accumulated fund as a tax free cash sum, unless you were over 45 or earning more than £60,000 at the date of the transfer. In these cases the maximum permitted cash sum may be less than 25% of the accumulated fund.

As with an ordinary personal pension plan, you will not be able to take any cash out of that part of the fund which represents your SERPS pension (the protected rights). This has to buy a special annuity, as described in Chapter 4, but the remainder of the fund may be used to buy whatever sort of annuity you wish. (See Chapter 4 for details).

The advantages of transferring to a personal pension plan are as follows:

- Possibility of good investment growth giving a better pension.

- Freedom to choose how you wish to have your pension paid.

- Possibly greater cash sum at retirement (if you were under 45 and earning less than £60,000).

- Flexibility of retirement age at any time between 50 and 75.

- Probability of greater benefits for your family if you die before retirement.

- Your own individual policy, free from the control of your previous employer.

The disadvantages of transferring are as follows:

- Transfer value may not represent good value for money.

- Lack of guarantees as to the pension payable.

- You have to take responsibility for choosing the personal
pension plan.

For some people who have decided to transfer, a special 'buy out'
policy may have more advantages than a personal pension plan.

A Buy out policy (sometimes still known as a 'Section 32 policy') is
similar to a personal pension plan in that the transfer value is paid to a
life assurance company. The amount of the benefits at retirement will
then depend on the performance of the life assurance company's
investments. However, the form in which those benefits are taken will
depend on the benefits you could have had under the rules of your
previous employer's scheme. This is quite different from transferring
to a personal pension plan (see page 51).

This is a highly complex area, and you should consult a specialist
pensions adviser before deciding between the two types of policy.

Member of a pension scheme moving to an employer who does not
have a pension scheme or becoming self-employed

You have the same options as in (1) and (3) (see page 49) above. You will
probably wish to take out a personal pension plan so that you can
continue to provide for your retirement, so it will probably make sense
to take a transfer to a personal pension plan.

Member of a pension scheme but not moving to another job

You have the same options as in (1) and (3) (see page 49) above.

Whether or not you decide to transfer from an employer's scheme to a
personal pension plan will depend on your age and how optimistic you
are about investment returns. If you are very close to your normal
retirement age under the scheme (say within five years), you will
probably wish to remain a member. If you are much younger, you will
probably prefer the added flexibility of the personal pension plan, and
having your own investment giving you growth which you can watch.
You will have to decide whether you prefer the guarantees offered by

a final salary scheme or the possibility that good investment returns will give you a higher pension.

Personal pension plan and moving to an employer with a pension scheme

You have three options open to you.

(1)   You can decide not to join your new employer's scheme and to continue your personal pension plan instead. This is similar to the situation described in Chapter 4.

        Remember that your new employer will probably be unwilling to contribute to your personal pension plan if he already operates a pension scheme which you have decided not to join. This option may make sense though if you do not expect to stay with this employer very long.

(2)   You can discontinue your personal pension plan and join the employer's scheme.

        If you do join the scheme, you will not be able to continue payments to your personal pension plan. If you stop making payments the contributions already paid grow until you retire.

(3)   You may transfer the value of your personal pension plan to your new employer's scheme, provided that the scheme is able to accept it.

If the new scheme is a final salary scheme, this transfer will enable you to exchange unknown future benefits for promised ones. However, it is difficult to know whether the extra benefits offered in exchange for the transfer represent good value for money. If they do, you may still lose out if you change jobs again and want to take a transfer value out of the scheme.

Unless you feel strongly that you would like to have the guarantees offered by a final salary scheme for this part of your pension, it is probably more sensible to keep the personal pension plan until retirement, even though you no longer contribute to it.

If the new scheme is a money purchase scheme, there is very little point in transferring the value of your personal pension plan. The money purchase scheme has much the same investment features as the personal pension plan, but it gives you much less flexibility at retirement.

Personal pension plan and moving to an employer without a scheme or becoming self-employed

Your personal pension plan is completely portable, so you may take it with you and continue it.

If you were employed and your employer was contributing, but you are now about to be self-employed you will probably need to increase your contributions if you are to receive your expected level of pension at retirement.

Personal pension plan and not moving to another job

As explained in Chapter 4, you may only contribute to a personal pension plan if you have net relevant earnings. If you have none in a tax year, you will have to cease payments to your plan. The value of the contributions already paid will continue to grow until you reach retirement age.

Chapter 2 describes some of the changes currently affecting pension schemes. Two of these in particular may have an effect on transfer values:

- If the scheme has a surplus which has to be used to improve leavers' benefits this will also improve transfer values.

- If the scheme does not already have the same retirement ages for men and women it will no longer be possible to treat them differently when they leave. This may improve transfer values.

Unless the scheme you are leaving already offers the same (or flexible) retirement ages for men and women, and already provides annual increases on pensions in payment, it may be better for you to delay taking your transfer value for the time being. The effects of the changes could result in its being substantially higher. On the other hand, you should remember that if you delay taking your transfer value for a year, you will lose a year's investment in your personal pension plan. Also, there could be a serious loss to your family should you die. Very few pension schemes will continue life assurance benefits once you have left.

Once the transfer payment is in the personal pension plan, 25% of the fund can be paid in cash if you die. The balance will be used to buy a widow or widower's pension. (If you do not leave a widow or widower, then the whole fund may be paid to your family.)

9

Other matters to consider

A pension mortgage is a loan to enable the borrower to purchase (or improve) a house. It differs from other types of mortgage because it is repayable out of the tax-free cash sum available from a pension scheme or personal pension plan when the borrower retires. Only interest is payable on the loan until it is repaid in full. The loan outstanding is also usually covered by life assurance to protect the position if the borrower should die before retirement.

A pension mortgage does not mean a loan given to you by a pension scheme or personal pension plan.

The advantages of a pension mortgage are set out briefly below:

- Lower outgoings than under a conventional mortgage (because tax relief is available against the pension premiums).

- Tax efficiency and flexibility.

- Favourable terms may be available.

- Loan not repayable until retirement.

The disadvantages are as follows:

- Unless you make other savings arrangements during your working life, the lump sum remaining after you have repaid the mortgage may reduce your post-retirement capital, and therefore income, below the level you need.

- Complications can arise if you leave your present employment.

- Unforeseen circumstances such as early retirement or redundancy can also cause problems.

Pension mortgages are usually readily available through retirement annuities and personal pension plans. A growing number of lenders will now make pension mortgage facilities available to members of pension schemes. Some employers are beginning to set up pension mortgage arrangements for members of their schemes, so it will be worth finding out whether your employer has done so, if you think a pension mortgage might suit you.

Gaps in normal employment

These gaps can arise, for example, if you are away from your employment through:

- disability e.g. a serious accident or illness;

- an overseas posting;

- maternity leave;

- enjoying a sabbatical or extended leave.

(a)   Pension schemes

The effect of the gap in your employment will depend on the trust deed and rules of your employer's pension scheme, but may have the following consequences:

- In a final salary scheme, the loss of that period of qualifying service for calculating your pension benefit on the 1/60th or 1/80th formula.

- In a money purchase scheme, the loss of contributions during the period of absence, which results in a smaller fund for the purchase of an annuity when you retire.

Your employers may be prepared to negotiate special arrangements with you. For assignments overseas, for example, they would be likely to continue to contribute to the pension scheme so that you do not suffer any loss of pension benefit or arrange for you to join an overseas scheme. There are plans to make it compulsory for employers to treat maternity leave as part of your pensionable service but no date for this has yet been mentioned.

(b)   Personal Pension Plans

You cannot contribute more than the maximum you are allowed in any tax year (see table on page 27). So if your earnings are lower because of your absence, your contribution for that tax year may have to be less.

Early retirement

Early retirement is not normally an option if you are aged less than 50.

(a)   Pension schemes

Retiring before the normal retirement age set under your employer's pension scheme's rules will normally reduce your pension benefits because:

- fewer contributions will have been paid into the scheme on your behalf by both employer and you;

- the cost of purchasing an annuity will be higher.

However, if you are retiring early at the request of your employer, e.g. through redundancy, you should expect to be able to negotiate a pension somewhere in value between the minimum one to which you are entitled now and that which you would have expected to receive had you continued in employment until normal retirement date.

Don't forget, since 17 May 1990 it has been illegal under European Community law to treat men and women differently if they retire early, but no one yet knows exactly how the new rules are going to apply.

(b)   Personal pension plan

Again, your pension will be less than expected at normal retirement date for the same reasons as set out above. If your employer is not contributing to your personal pension plan he will be unlikely to offer any financial help to improve that pension.

Late retirement

(*a*) **Pension schemes**

You may wish, or be asked, to continue to be employed beyond your normal retirement age as laid down by the pension scheme. Whether you or your employer will continue to make contributions to the scheme on your behalf will depend on the rules and trust deed of the scheme. If no further contributions are to be paid, you will normally have the following options (subject to the rules of the scheme):

(1) To draw your benefits and continue working. If you do this you will be eligible to pay contributions to a personal pension plan (unless you were a controlling director; see page 26).

(2) To defer your benefits until you actually retire. In this event your benefits should be increased because of your late retirement.

(3) To draw your tax-free cash sum and defer your pension (but not if you joined the scheme since March 1987).

(*b*) **Personal pension plans**

You can continue to contribute to these up to the age of 75, at which time you must draw your benefits. If you wish, you may draw all or some of your existing benefits and still continue contributing. This might be attractive if you were to continue earning, but at a lower level than before.

Death in service

(*a*) **Pension schemes**

Your employer's pension scheme is likely to provide protection for you and your dependants by one of the following:

- Life assurance cover - a tax-free lump sum usually equal to a multiple of gross annual salary (up to the Inland Revenue maximum of 4 x gross annual pay).

- A widow or widower's pension - often equal to one-half (or some other proportion up to the Inland Revenue maximum of two-thirds) of the pension you would have received under the pension scheme's rules had you remained in your present job (at your rate of pay at the date of death) until your normal retirement age.

If the scheme does not provide the maximum death in service cover permitted by the Inland Revenue and you feel that what is provided is inadequate, then you can use an AVC to provide additional cover.

(b)   Personal pension plans

Most personal pension plans pay a return on death equivalent to the fund built up by the contributions paid up to the date of death. Obviously, this fund may be quite substantial towards the end of a working life, but is unlikely to be adequate if you have just started the plan.

You may use up to 5% of your earnings each year to provide life assurance cover. You will receive full tax relief against the premiums paid for life cover under a personal pension plan in the same way as you do for contributions paid to provide pension. However, this 5% forms part of your maximum percentage of earnings, as described on page 26. You cannot make the maximum permitted pension contribution and pay for personal pension life cover as well.

If you wish to use the whole of your maximum contribution to provide pension, you will have to use an ordinary life assurance policy to provide death in service cover. The exception to this is if your employer provides death in service benefits for you.

Death after retirement

(a)   Pension schemes

Many pension schemes now guarantee your pension for five years after it begins, whether or not you are alive. For example, if you die one year after your pension has begun, another four years' worth of pension will be payable. Often this is paid in a lump sum and may be discounted for early payment.

Most pension schemes will also pay your widow or widower a pension for the remainder of her or his life. Schemes vary as to what they provide, but the amount normally relates to the pension you were receiving at the date of your death e.g. one-half or two-thirds of that pension.

Increases in pensions made by your pension scheme after you retire would also usually be applied to widow's or widower's pensions.

(b)   Personal pension plans

The protection provided for your widow or widower will depend on the type of pension you select at retirement (see page 29).

Reducing your pension to provide extra widow's or widower's pension

Some pension schemes will allow you to decide at the time of your retirement to take a lower pension yourself for the rest of your life so that after your death your spouse can receive a pension or a higher pension for the remainder of her or his life.

The position under a personal pension plan will depend on the type of pension you select at retirement (see page 29).

The earnings cap

As explained in Chapter 4, the Finance Act 1989 restricted the amount of earnings which may be pensioned. For a pension scheme, whether final salary or money purchase, the benefits at retirement must not exceed Inland Revenue limits. Since 1989 these limits are based on the amount of the cap, not on your actual salary if that is higher than the cap.

For a personal pension plan, the maximum percentage which you may contribute is a percentage of the cap, not of your actual earnings if they are higher. This applies to all personal pension plans, whether you are employed or self-employed, to all new pension schemes, and to all individuals who join existing pension schemes (unless they joined before June 1989).

The earnings cap was introduced in March 1989 and set at £60,000 for the year ending 5 April 1990. The figure is to increase each year in line with inflation. So for the year ending 5 April 1991 it is £64,800 and for the year ending 5 April 1992 it is £71,400.

You will probably feel that this figure is set so high that the problem is unlikely ever to affect you, but there is a point to remember. The cap increases each year in line **with inflation in prices**, not in line with increases in **national average earnings**. In the past, **earnings** have grown more quickly than **prices**.

The table in Appendix A shows how much more significant inflation can be at 9% compared with 3%.

What you can do

If you are thinking of changing your job and it is possible that, either immediately or in the future, your earnings will exceed the cap, you should raise the matter with your prospective employer when you are discussing your terms of employment. It may be very much more difficult to negotiate special arrangements once you have taken the job.

This is one situation in which it may be better to have a personal pension plan instead of joining your employer's scheme. The personal pension plan may give you higher benefits at retirement, particularly if you have already accrued substantial benefits from previous employers.

If you do find yourself in this position and are discussing pension provision with a new employer, he may be willing to compensate you for not being able to expect pension benefits based on your full salary. He may offer you one or more of the following:

●   A promise that you will receive a pension at retirement over and above what you can expect from the pension scheme or personal pension plan.

- A pension from a scheme which is not approved by the Inland Revenue and so does not receive the favourable tax treatment of an approved pension scheme. In this case, you will have to pay income tax on the employer's contributions to the scheme as you do on every other taxable benefit in kind.

- Extra salary to enable you to make additional provision for your retirement through private savings (see Chapter 10).

- Other benefits, such as share option schemes which give you the opportunity to acquire shares in your employing company on favourable terms and so benefit from its future growth.

10
Private savings

The pension route

All pension schemes, personal pension plans and retirement annuities have certain features in common. They all offer the following benefits:

- Tax relief on contributions.

- No tax on income or capital gains on the investments of the scheme or plan.

- A guaranteed income in retirement.

- A tax-free cash sum at retirement.

- Possible protection to dependants in case of death in service (in most pension schemes).

- Protection for the investments: they belong neither to your employer nor to you.

- The opportunity to avoid inheritance tax if you die before you retire.

If you are a member of a pension scheme you will enjoy all these advantages. If you are not a member of a scheme, whether because you have decided not to join or because you are self-employed, you should use a personal pension plan to provide yourself with a sensible pension at retirement. However, many people will at some time during their working lives wish to make some extra savings. There are many different types of investment available, and many advisers ready to recommend them. Which is the best investment?

There is no 'best' investment. The most suitable investment for you will depend on your personal circumstances; for instance, how long you wish to leave your money invested and your attitude to risk. These will in turn be affected by how much you wish to save.

The first question you should ask yourself is:

What am I saving for?

If the answer is that you are saving for your retirement, because you want a better pension, then if you are a member of a scheme you should consider AVCs.

You may feel that you would prefer a wider selection than you have under your employer's AVC scheme or schemes. If you do, then you should consider an FSAVC, but don't forget that you will have to meet the charges involved yourself. Under the AVC scheme, your employer will pay most of the charges.

If you want to improve your pension but you are not a member of a pension scheme, then you should increase your contributions to a personal pension plan (provided that you are not already paying the maximum). You could choose a different pension provider, particularly if you would like a higher risk investment for your 'extra' savings.

If you are saving for retirement, but you want to improve the cash sum you will need, there will be little point in using an AVC or FSAVC, since you cannot take any cash out of them at retirement. (A personal pension plan will allow you to take up to 25% of the accumulated fund at retirement as a cash sum.)

If you are saving to provide extra cash at retirement, or you do not wish to wait until you retire to have the benefit of your savings, then you will need to consider alternatives to AVCs, FSAVCs or personal pension plans. This is also true if you are already making your maximum permissible pension contributions, particularly if your earnings are subject to the 'earnings cap'.

The non-pensions route

All the investments considered under this heading can be used for monthly savings. The first important thing to remember is that none of them will give you tax relief on contributions as all your private savings have to be made out of your after tax income. If you pay £75 to an AVC, FSAVC or personal pension plan, the scheme or plan provider will invest £100 on your behalf. With any private savings, if you pay £75, £75 is the amount invested.

Personal Equity Plans (PEPs)

PEPs were designed to encourage more people to invest in equities (company shares). You may choose a plan which invests in a few selected shares, or one which invests in *unit trusts**, or one which combines the two.

> *A *unit trust* invests in a spread of different stocks and shares, and issues you with **units** instead of actual shares. In this way, you can benefit from the growth of a number of companies, even if your personal investment is small. (See Chapter 4 for description of unit-linked pension funds which work on a similar principle.)

You do not receive tax relief on your contributions to a PEP, but you pay no income tax or capital gains tax on the investments within the PEP. You may withdraw an income tax-free and cash in the investment without paying capital gains tax.

Because of the tax advantages, the government limits the amount you may invest in a PEP. For the tax year ending April 1992, the maximum you may invest in a unit trust PEP is £250 per month (or £3,000 as a lump sum) and in a share-based or share and unit-trust PEP the amount is £500 per month (or £6,000 as a lump sum). These figures are   the amounts which you may actually invest. The charges involved in setting up the PEP may be paid in addition.

The 1991 Budget proposals introduced a third type of PEP. Up to £3,000 per annum may now be invested in a single-share (Corporate) PEP in addition to the limits mentioned in the preceding paragraph.

You could consider combining a PEP and an AVC (or FSAVC). The PEP will provide additional cash at retirement (or sooner, if you need it); the AVC will pay additional pension.

You must remember that, whatever type of PEP you choose, your investment will be in equities. This means it will be a high risk investment. The rewards should be high as well, but the value will vary from time to time, following the movements of the stock market. It is not a suitable short term investment.

Savings-related share option scheme

Some employers offer you the opportunity to buy shares in the company you work for on favourable terms.

You agree to save a fixed monthly amount for five or seven years in a special savings account with a building society or other deposit organisation. This account gives you a guaranteed rate of interest which is added to your account tax-free at the end of five, or seven, years.

You may then either cash in the savings account without any penalty, or use it to buy the shares which your employer has set aside for you. You will buy them at the price for which they were bought and sold when the scheme started, not the price on the day you buy them.

You are then free to keep the shares to enjoy further growth or to sell them. You may have to pay *capital gains tax** when you sell them.

Capital gains tax for an individual is payable when your real gains (i.e. the growth in your investment above and beyond inflation) are more than £5,500 in one tax year. You do not have to pay it until you actually sell the investment and 'realise' the gain. In order to work out the **rate** of tax you have to pay, the gain you have made is added to your income for that tax year. Depending on your income, therefore, capital gains tax at the moment is either 25% or 40%.

You should remember that, if you decide to keep the shares, you are making an equity investment. Unlike the PEP, which gives you the opportunity to invest in a spread of shares in different companies, a share option scheme involves only shares in the company which employs you. However, another 1991 Budget Proposals exempts shares from capital gains tax if they are transferred to a single-share (Corporate) PEP (see page 66).

Because of the tax advantages, you may not pay more than £250 a month into the savings account.

Life assurance policy

A life assurance policy may be a suitable investment, provided you are prepared to save for a period of years. To obtain the best results, you need to pay premiums for ten years.

You will not receive any tax relief against your premiums, but you will receive the cash sum at the end of ten years tax free. In the meantime, your investments will not have been tax-free: the life assurance company has to pay tax on its non-pension funds, but at a rate approximately the same as the **basic** rate of tax (currently 25%). This is a tax advantage if you would pay higher rate tax (currently 40%) on your own investments, but does not help if you are a basic rate taxpayer.

A life assurance policy does have two advantages however:

- Access to a wide range of investments, including with profits, (see pages 32-34) which is not available from any other type of investment.

- Benefit for your family on death. You can use the policy to provide additional life assurance cover as well as an investment, though the higher the life assurance the lower will be the investment portion and *vice versa*. You can also arrange the policy so that, if you die the proceeds can be paid to your family immediately, and there will be no inheritance tax to pay.

Tax Exempt Special Savings Accounts (TESSAs)

These accounts were introduced in the Finance Act 1990 to encourage savings, and are available from 1 January 1991. They represent the safest form of saving. They will only be available from banks and building societies, since they are a deposit type investment (see page 31).

The maximum total investment is £9,000 over a five-year period, so the maximum monthly investment is £150. (Alternatively, you may invest a lump sum of £3,000 in the first year, followed by £1,800 in each of the next three years and £600 in the fifth year.) You should aim to keep the investment for the full five years. Provided that you do so, interest on the account will build up gross and you will pay no tax on it.

This type of investment is very safe, but it does not offer any genuine capital growth. The money you invest will not fall in value, but it will not grow either, apart from the income (interest) which is being saved up within the investment.

None of these investments offers the same degree of tax efficiency and security as an AVC, FSAVC or personal pension plan, but they are not tied to your retirement and you can withdraw the investment much sooner i.e. after five, seven, ten years or at any time.

The main questions you have to ask yourself are:

How long do I wish to save for?

How much risk am I prepared to take?

Once you have answered them, you may feel able to decide which type of savings arrangement will suit you. If you feel you would like more advice, then you should talk to an independent financial adviser (see page 78). Avoid a representative who is 'tied' to recommending the products of only one organisation since that particular organisation may not offer the full range of savings schemes. Even if it does, it is unlikely to be the best in each category.

11

How to decide what to do

You now have to choose between the alternatives available to you in your category of employment as explained in Chapter 3.

This chapter contains some unbiased, independent advice and guidance to help you make that important decision.

Basic principles

Before considering the specific choices you can make, there are some basic principles worth remembering:

(1)   The more you pay in, the more you get out

That sounds obvious (and is). The point to be made, though, is that pension schemes, AVC schemes, FSAVC schemes and personal pension plans should all achieve broadly the same rate of investment return (interest, dividends and capital growth) as they all enjoy the same exemptions from tax on their income and on capital gains made from the sale of their investments.

Therefore, the greater the contributions that are made to a scheme or plan, the higher the benefits should be at retirement.

(2)   For the majority it will be better to remain a member of, or to join, your employer's pension scheme

The main reasons are as follows:

● Your employer will be making contributions (often substantial) to the pension scheme for your and other members' benefit. Not many employers will wish to contribute towards personal pension plans when they already offer a final salary or money purchase scheme.

- The pension scheme usually also provides other valuable benefits such as life assurance, widow's or widower's pensions etc. These benefits will cost you additional contributions if you provide them under a personal pension plan (see Chapter 9).

- The pension scheme has the employer's backing. In final salary schemes, the employer undertakes to make whatever contributions are necessary to provide the 'defined benefits'.

- Expenses of the pension schemes are usually met by the employer. On personal pensions there will be deductions from the amount invested to meet commission and charges.

- Contributions will be adjusted automatically as your earnings increase. Under a personal pension plan you have the sole responsibility for making sure that you review your contributions from time to time to keep them on a realistic basis (although a good adviser will remind you).

However, there are some exceptions to this general rule, as explained on page 73.

(3)   Investment returns are very important

Pension scheme actuaries sometimes tell employers that, as a 'rule of thumb' an annual improvement of 1% (i.e. say from 7% to 8% in the rate of return from investments, interest, dividends and capital gains) can mean a reduction of as much as 20% in the contributions required to meet benefits in final salary schemes. Alternatively - and preferably from your point of view as a member - the improved finances of the pension scheme can be used to increase scheme benefits.

As explained in Chapter 2, an **employer will no longer be able to stop contributing or take a refund** if there is a surplus in the scheme, until he has arranged to give all pensions the benefit of limited price indexation.

In money purchase schemes or in a retirement annuity or personal pension plan, the rates of investment return are equally important. The sum available at your retirement will increase if the rate of investment return rises. For example, £1,000 p.a. paid in monthly instalments for 20 years will be worth £47,400 if it grows at 8% a year compound and £53,200 if it grows at 9% a year compound.

(4)   Pensions are only part of your lifetime financial needs

Your decision on your future method of providing for your pension should not be taken in isolation.

Your decision may be affected, for example, by factors such as:

- your partner's (i.e. husband, wife etc.) income and pension expectations;

- your own and your partner's investments or other 'private' income;

- the need to provide for heavy family expenses in the immediate future;

- your own and your partner's health;

- how secure you feel in your present employment; and

- your life assurance policies or other pension expectations from previous employment.

Decisions to be taken

The choices available to you were explained in Chapter 3. Your decisions can be reduced to four.

(1)   Should you rely only on the State schemes ?

(2)   If you are already a member of (or can join) a pension scheme, should you opt out in favour of a personal pension plan?

(3)   Should you contract-out of SERPS (if you have that option)?

(4)   Are AVCs worthwhile for you?

(1)   Should you rely only on the State schemes ?

Almost certainly not. Chapter 7 indicates the pension you can expect from the State flat-rate scheme and from SERPS.

It is most unlikely that these two schemes alone will provide you with sufficient income to meet your needs in retirement.

Relying on the State schemes alone is not recommended.

(2)   Pension scheme or Personal pension plan?

If you are already a member (or are eligible to join) a pension scheme, should you opt out in favour of a personal pension plan? Three main reasons to favour a pension scheme rather than a personal pension plan were given earlier in this Chapter (see pages 70 and 71).

Some people will have little difficulty in deciding. For example, if you are aged 45, in a good scheme and expecting to remain in service up to retirement, there is little point in taking a personal pension. If you have a significant period of past service as well, the case is even more convincing.

On the other hand, if you are in your early twenties, optimistic about investment prospects and expecting to leave your current employment in a year or so, then the personal pension is likely to offer the better choice. This is particularly true if you expect to change jobs fairly frequently during your working life. The only exceptions will be if the pension scheme is a money purchase scheme or provides that its benefits, even for early leavers, will be as good as those from a money purchase scheme.

The table on page 76 sets out the particular circumstances or factors which you should also take into account in deciding whether to opt out of a pension scheme into a personal pension plan or vice versa.

(3)   Should you contract-out of SERPS?

Remember that you can only use an appropriate personal pension plan to contract-out of SERPS if you are employed but not a member of a pension scheme which is already contracted-out.

The main factors to consider in making this decision are set out in the following table, which shows the effect of each of them.

	Favours an appropriate personal pension plan or FSAVC	Favours SERPS
Your age	Younger	Older
Expected investment returns	Optimistic	Pessimistic
Entitled to 2% incentive	Yes	No

The advice offered on SERPS is based on the **present** position. At the moment there is an incentive available to people who contract out of SERPS using an appropriate personal pension plan. Until April 1993 this is 2% of band earnings (see page 25).

In 1993 both the incentive and the contracting out rebate (see pages 24 and 25) will be reviewed. The National Audit Office, whose job is to monitor government expenditure and comment on its efficiency, has just produced a report on SERPS. The report suggests that the costs involved in encouraging people to contract out of SERPS are higher than was expected when compared with the probable costs of SERPS itself.

This means that both the rebate and the incentive may well be reduced from 1993. This will affect the ages at which it is sensible to opt out of SERPS using an appropriate personal pension, making them lower than they are at present.

IN OR OUT OF SERPS

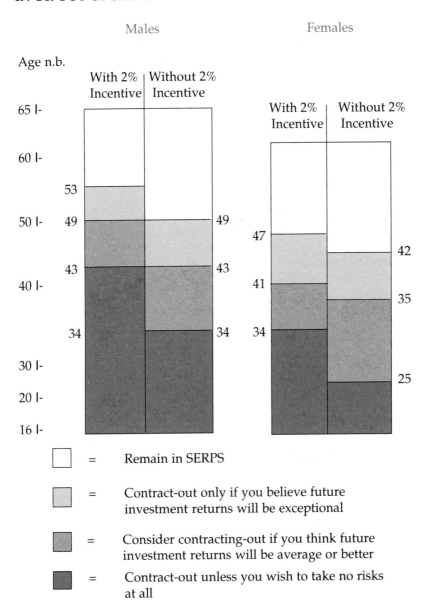

Caution: These table are only valid until 6 April 1993. (This assumes that there are no changes before this date.)

	Favours a Pension scheme	Favours a personal pension plan
Your age	Older	Younger
Expectation of leaving present employment	Low	High
Expectation about investment returns	Pessimistic	Optimistic
Expectation about your future pay increases	Faster than average	Slower than average
Level of employee contributions to pension scheme	Low	High
Past service rights in present pension scheme	Long service	Short service
Need to provide for dependants	High	Low
Extent to which you are prepared to take trouble to make own pension arrangements	Little extent	Great extent
Level of benefits in the pension scheme	Good	Poor
Entitled to the 2% incentive for a personal pension plan	No	Yes

(4)   Are AVCs worthwhile for you?

The features of AVCs and FSAVCs, and some of their advantages and disadvanages, were explained in Chapter 5. You will recall that you may only make AVCs or FSAVCs if you are a member of a pension scheme.

Examples of when you should consider paying AVCs or FSAVCs.

- If your pension scheme will not provide you with the maximum pension permitted by the Inland Revenue for your length of service with that employer.

- If your pension benefits are calculated on basic salary only, so that earnings from overtime, bonus or commission are not included.

- If your 'pensionable salary' from the scheme is not your full salary. For instance, it is quite common for final salary pension schemes to exclude the amount of the lower band earnings (£52 per week = £2,704 per year from April 1991 to April 1992).

- If your employer's pension scheme does not provide an increasing pension in retirement. (This is more likely to apply to money purchase schemes after the Social Security Act 1990 has come into force.)

Examples of when AVCs or FSAVCs are not recommended.

- If your pension from your pension scheme is already nearing the maximum allowed by the Inland Revenue.

- If you are young - say 35 or under - because money put into AVC policies cannot be obtained by you until you retire.

- If you are anxious to maximise your lump sum at retirement. New AVCs and FSAVCs can now only be used to improve pension benefits. Your pension scheme may well not take your AVC or FSAVC pension into account when calculating your maximum cash entitlement.

One final point on AVCs. You need not be concerned about whether you will still be able to afford an AVC once started. You may vary the amount and timing of AVCs as you wish, subject to the overriding Inland Revenue limitations.

AVCs and FSAVCs are compared with other forms of saving in Chapter 10.

Conclusion

It will be clear from what you have read already that pensions in the UK have become an immensely complex subject and one on which it is never possible to say the last word. At the time of writing we are still waiting for the following developments to occur:

- The date from which pension scheme surpluses must be used to provide Limited Price Indexation (LPI).

- How to work out whether a scheme has a surplus or not.

- The setting up of the Pensions Registry.

- Full details of the Ombudsman's powers.

- Clarification of the new rules laid down in the Barber case.

- The government's review of the basis for contracting-out of SERPS which may affect both the amount of the rebate and the incentive.

If, after reading this book, you want further advice, you are recommended to talk first to the pensions expert at your place of employment or to the firm (consulting actuaries or pensions consultants) which advises your employers on pensions matters. Local accountants or solicitors now often have someone who is knowledgeable on pensions matters.

If you do decide to take out a personal pension, either because you are self-employed or because your employer does not offer a pension scheme (or he does, but you wish to opt out of it) or because you are changing jobs, you should obtain independent advice.

You should consult an insurance broker or other adviser who is authorised under the Financial Services Act 1986 through FIMBRA (the Financial Intermediaries Managers and Brokers Regulatory Association) or IMRO (the Investment Managers Regulatory Organisation). An accountant or solicitor may not be authorised under the Act to advise you on which plan to choose. However, he could well be able to recommend an independent adviser for you to consult.

You can also obtain advice about a suitable consultant from the following organisation:

Society of Pension Consultants
Ludgate House
Ludgate Circus
London
EC4A 2AB

Appendix A

Effect of inflation

Both the purchasing power of the ultimate benefit and the real cost of contributions payable will depend on the rate of inflation over the period of the plan. By way of illustration the following table shows what £1,000 will be worth in today's money at the end of the periods shown if the annual rate of inflation over the period is as shown:

Period (years)	Purchasing power of £1,000		
	3% Inflation	6% Inflation	9% Inflation
5	863	747	650
10	744	588	422
15	642	417	275
20	554	312	178
25	478	233	116
30	412	174	75
35	355	130	49
40	307	97	32

Source: The Rulebook of the Securities and Investment Board

Retirement annuities

Since July 1988 it is no longer possible to take out a new retirement annuity (formerly called a **section 226 policy**). However, there is nothing to prevent you from continuing with an existing one. Some retirement annuities will permit you to make additional contributions, either by paying increased monthly or annual premiums or by single payments.

Retirement annuities are very similar to personal pension plans, which replaced them. There is no limit on the benefits which you may draw: the limit is on the percentage of your earnings which you may contribute.

Retirement annuities differ from personal pension plans in the following ways:

- They cannot be used to contract-out of SERPS.

- The pension cannot be taken before age 60 or later than age 75 (50 and 75 for personal pension plans).

- They cannot accept transfers from pension schemes or personal pension plans.

- The maximum tax-free cash sum at retirement is not 25% of the fund. It is calculated using a complicated formula so that the cash you draw is not more than three times the remaining pension. This means that the older you are when you draw your benefits, the higher you can expect your cash to be. It will also be higher if annuity rates are high when you take your pension. Broadly speaking, you may expect the cash sum to be between 25% and 35% of the value of the policy.

- The maximum contributions, which are set out below, are lower as a percentage of earnings than for a personal pension plan.

Age at start of the tax year (6 April)	% of earnings
Up to 50	17.5
51 to 55	20.0
56 to 60	22.5
61 to 74	27.5

Notes:

(a)   You may pay up to 5% out of these percentages to provide **life assurance cover,** as you may with a personal pension.

(b)   The percentages are percentages of **total** earnings, not capped earnings. If you are earning in excess of the cap (currently £71,400, but see Chapter 9), and you have a retirement annuity policy able to accept your contributions, you may be able to pay a higher sum into the retirement annuity than into a personal pension plan. However, you will not be able to take advantage of this if you have already made a payment to a personal pension plan for that tax year.

Glossary

Annuity: an income for life provided by an insurance company in exchange for a non-returnable capital sum.

Appropriate personal pension plan: one which satisfies certain conditions under the Social Security Act 1986 and is approved by the Occupational Pensions Board, which enables the contributor to the plan to be contracted-out of SERPS.

Approved pension scheme: one which meets certain requirements of the Inland Revenue, and which therefore enjoys the tax privileges outlined on pages 6 and 7.

AVCs: additional voluntary contributions by a member of a pension scheme to increase a pension at retirement.

Band earnings: pay between the lower and upper earnings limits for national insurance (between £52 and £390 per week for 1991/92).

Buy out policy: the option on leaving a pension scheme to transfer preserved benefits to an insurance company of your choice. Still sometimes known as Section 32 buy-outs after the legislation which first made available this choice.

Contracted-in pension scheme: one whose members have not been contracted-out of SERPS.

Contracted-out pension scheme: one whose members have been contracted-out of SERPS, by being an approved scheme which satisfied certain conditions laid down by the Occupational Pensions Board.

Contributory pension scheme: one to which both employer and members are required to make contributions, usually as a percentage of pay.

Glossary

Defined benefit pension scheme: one under which the pension benefits at retirement are fixed (usually as 1/60th or 1/80th of final pensionable pay for each year of pensionable service), with the employer undertaking to make whatever contributions are necessary in addition to any members' contributions (which are usually a fixed percentage of pensionable pay). Also known as **'final salary' scheme.**

Defined contribution scheme: one to which contributions by either or both employer and members are at agreed rates, the ultimate benefits being dependent on the size of the fund built-up, annuity rates at retirement dates, etc. Also known as **'money purchase' scheme.**

Final salary scheme: see Defined benefit pension scheme.

Free-standing AVCs: additional voluntary contributions by a member of a pension scheme to an insurance policy or building society outside the pension scheme.

Guaranteed minimum pension (GMP): the minimum level of pension which a pension scheme has to provide in order for its members to be contracted-out of SERPS.

In-scheme AVCs: additional voluntary contributions by a member of a pension scheme to an insurance policy or building society chosen by his or her pension scheme or to the scheme itself.

Leaving service: leaving an employer's employment for any reason.

Money purchase scheme: see Defined contribution scheme.

Net relevant earnings: earnings from employment or as a self-employed person, less deductions (other than personal allowances) which are made to determine an individual's net income for tax purposes.

Non-contributory pension scheme: one to which only the employer makes contributions.

Pensionable salary (or pay): the pay on which a scheme member's pension will be based.

Pensionable service: employment which counts as years of service towards a member's benefit entitlement from a pension scheme.

Pension mortgages: a mortgage on which the principal (i.e. loan) is repaid out of lump sums which become available on retirement from pension arrangements of the borrower.

Pension scheme: in this book means any occupational pension scheme, i.e. one provided for employees by an employer, or a scheme open to employees within a certain trade or profession (e.g. the Social Workers' Pension Fund).

Personal pension/personal pension plan: new pension arrangement introduced under the Social Security Act 1986 and Finance Act (No 2) 1987. Enables an employee or self-employed person to make contributions to his or her own pension plan (see Chapter 4).

Retirement annuity: the forerunner of the personal pension plan. No longer available, but existing contributions may be continued or in some cases increased. Still sometimes known as Section 226 policies, a reference to the Income and Corporation Taxes Act 1970.

Revalued average band earnings: band earnings revalued in line with national earnings levels each year.

Section 226 policy: see Retirement annuity.

Section 32 buy-out: see Buy out policy

SERPS: the State Earnings Related Pension Scheme which provides an additional pension based on pay in band earnings.

Index

*= term defined in Glossary